LIFE IN A RIVER

LIFE IN A RIVER

VALERIE RAPP

Lerner Publications Company
Minneapolis

To Sarah, Leah, and Adam Skrine. May your lives
be full of love, adventure, and joy. Love, Val

Lerner Publications Company
A division of Lerner Publishing Group
241 First Avenue North
Minneapolis, MN 55401 U.S.A.

Website address: www.lernerbooks.com

Library of Congress Cataloging-in-Publication Data

Rapp, Valerie.
    Life in a river / by Valerie Rapp.
        p.   cm.   — (Ecosystems in action)
    ISBN: 0–8225–2136–9 (lib. bdg. : alk. paper)
    1. Stream ecology—Columbia River Watershed—Juvenile literature. [1. Columbia
River Watershed. 2. Stream ecology. 3. Ecology.] I. Title. II. Series.
QH104.5.C64 2003
577.6'4'09795—dc21   2001001691

Manufactured in the United States of America
1 2 3 4 5 6 – JR – 08 07 06 05 04 03

CONTENTS

INTRODUCTION
WHAT IS AN ECOSYSTEM?

An ecosystem is a community of plants, animals, other living organisms, and their nonliving environment—including climate, soil, water, and air. All ecosystems, such as rivers, pine forests, deserts, and prairies, have three main elements: structures, functions, and composition.

Structures are the physical parts of an ecosystem that we can see and touch. In a forest ecosystem, the trees are one of the structures. In a river ecosystem, deep pools, side channels, and driftwood logs are three important structures. These structures create places that have fast currents and quiet pools. They create places with deep water and shallow water, and places that are rocky and other places that are sandy. All these different places in a river are called habitats, places where plants, animals, or other living organisms can live and grow.

Functions are the activities and processes that go on in an ecosystem. Functions include birth, growth, reproduction, death, and decay. Although the same functions take place in every ecosystem, they are carried out by different species in different ecosystems.

Composition refers to the different species of plants, animals, fungi, and bacteria that live in an ecosystem. The Columbia River ecosystem of western North America, for example, has many species of insects, mammals, fish, amphibians, and birds. The plants and animals found in an ecosystem are all adapted to their specific environment.

Organisms need energy to live. Scientists call the path of energy in an ecosystem the food chain. In any ecosystem that receives sunlight, the energy starts with the sun. The sun provides the energy that nearly all primary producers need to make food. Primary producers are mostly green plants, such as trees in a forest. Trees and all green plants are able to change sunlight to chemical energy. Then plants produce simple sugars and other foods that they need to grow. Primary consumers—animals such as rabbits or snails—eat the plants. Secondary consumers, also called predators, eat the plant-eating animals. Two predators are hawks and otters. Decomposers, such as bacteria and fungi, break down dead plants and animals into simple nutrients. These nutrients are used again by plants.

The Columbia River is the fourth largest river in North America, but it is only the eighteenth largest river in the world. Other rivers such as the Amazon River in Brazil and the Yangtze River in China are much longer than the Columbia and carry more water.

Other big rivers around the world have ecosystems that are different from the Columbia's—these other rivers have different species of plants, fish, insects, mammals, amphibians, and birds. But wherever they are found, rivers carry water from the mountains to the oceans. Rivers are closely connected to the land, whether they flow through forests, jungles, or grasslands. All rivers have floods. And in all rivers, living things are growing, eating, giving birth, and dying. The path of energy follows the path of the water—always flowing downhill, always moving.

ALL ECOSYSTEMS, SUCH AS RIVERS, PINE FORESTS, DESERTS, AND PRAIRIES, HAVE THREE MAIN ELEMENTS: STRUCTURES, FUNCTIONS, AND COMPOSITION.

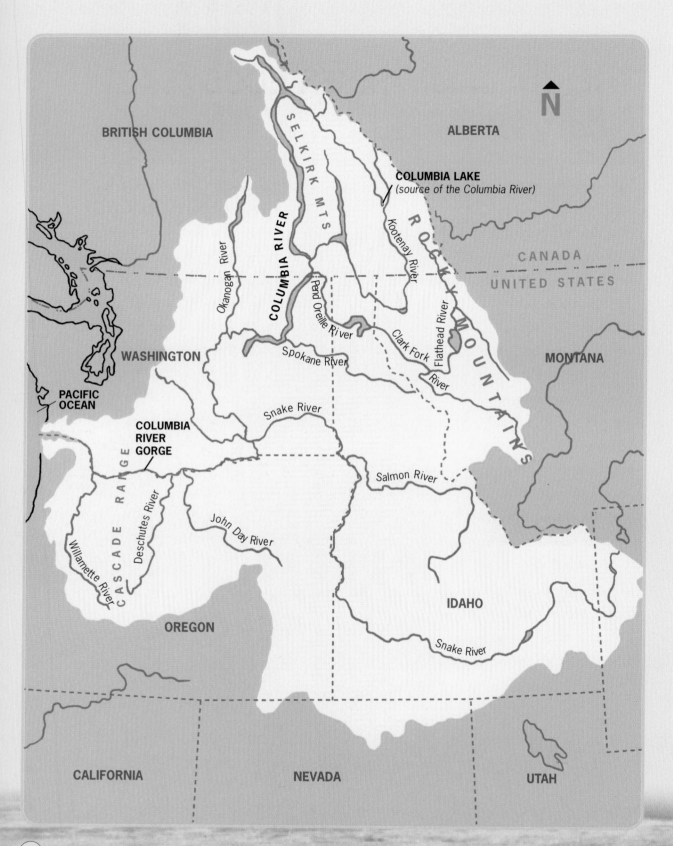

BRITISH COLUMBIA

ALBERTA

N

SELKIRK MTS

COLUMBIA RIVER

COLUMBIA LAKE
(source of the Columbia River)

Kootenay River

ROCKY MOUNTAINS

CANADA

UNITED STATES

Okanogan River

Pend Oreille River

Clark Fork River

Flathead River

WASHINGTON

Spokane River

MONTANA

PACIFIC OCEAN

Snake River

COLUMBIA RIVER GORGE

CASCADE RANGE

Salmon River

Deschutes River

John Day River

Willamette River

IDAHO

OREGON

Snake River

CALIFORNIA

NEVADA

UTAH

CHAPTER 1

THE COLUMBIA RIVER ECOSYSTEM:
A NATURAL HISTORY

High in the mountains, water begins to ripple, flow, and move in a small stream. The cold, clear freshwater tumbles over logs and drops over small waterfalls. Coming out of the mountains into a valley, the stream flows into Columbia Lake in the Canadian Rocky Mountains. The lake feeds into a river at its lower end, and the Columbia River begins. The river flows north through a valley between the Rocky Mountains and the Selkirk Mountains. At the north end of this valley, the Columbia makes a sharp turn to the south and comes back down the other side of the Selkirks.

Eventually the river flows into the United States in the state of Washington. Here the Columbia starts heading west to the Pacific Ocean, but it is blocked by the Cascade Mountains. The river flows south along the eastern slope of the Cascades. Just before the Columbia turns to flow toward the ocean again, the Snake River, which flows from Wyoming and Idaho, joins it. Soon after the Columbia and Snake join, the Columbia turns west toward the Pacific Ocean. From here to the ocean,

COLUMBIA LAKE, BRITISH COLUMBIA, THE SOURCE OF THE COLUMBIA RIVER

the Columbia River marks the border between the states of Washington and Oregon. The Columbia flows west, eventually running through a deep canyon in the Cascades called the Columbia Gorge. For the last 60 miles (100 kilometers) until it reaches the ocean, the river flows past the mountains of the Coast Ranges in Oregon and Washington.

The Columbia River gets wider as it nears the ocean. Its freshwater begins to mix with the saltwater pushed in by the tides, and the river's level goes up and down slightly with the tides. The part of the river where the saltwater and freshwater mix is called an estuary. By the time the river reaches the ocean, it is more than 5 miles (8 kilometers) wide. The Columbia River pours its water— more than 2 million gallons (7,600,000 liters) every second—into the ocean.

BY THE TIME THE RIVER REACHES THE OCEAN, IT IS MORE THAN 5 MILES (8 KILOMETERS) WIDE. THE COLUMBIA RIVER POURS ITS WATER— MORE THAN 2 MILLION GALLONS (7,600,000 LITERS) EVERY SECOND— INTO THE OCEAN.

Once known as the Great River of the West, the Columbia is more than 1,200 miles (1,900 kilometers) long. The Columbia flows past lightly populated lands—through pine and fir forests, sagebrush plains, lakes, and deep canyons. It also flows past wheat fields, orchards, nuclear power plants, aluminum factories, and cities. People have built many dams along the river. Reservoirs form behind the dams. Highways and railroads follow the river for much of its path.

The Columbia River is millions of years old. All the events of the past have created the landscape that we see in modern times as we follow the Columbia through the Pacific Northwest—states including Washington and Oregon, and the province of British Columbia in Canada. Flowing water erodes, or wears away, soil and rock, changing their shape or cutting through them. Over millions of years, the Columbia has eroded parts of the mountains it ran over. In eastern Washington, the river cut through lava flows thousands of feet thick, creating deep canyons. The Columbia also eroded a channel through the Cascade Mountains, creating the Columbia Gorge canyon. At least twice, lava flows from volcanoes in the Cascades completely blocked the Columbia Gorge, but the Columbia eroded through them.

During the last ice age, which began about seventy thousand years ago and ended about fifteen thousand years ago, much of the Northern Hemisphere was covered with glaciers, or large sheets of ice. The glaciers forced the course of the Columbia to change several times. One glacier blocked the river in northern Washington, forcing it to take a different route. In its new route, the river created much of Grand Coulee, a deep canyon in northern Washington. When the glacier melted, the Columbia returned to its old channel.

As the ice age was ending, another glacier blocked the rivers of northern Idaho. A huge lake formed behind the ice dam. When the lake rose high enough, the ice

ROWENA DELL, A VALLEY IN THE COLUMBIA RIVER GORGE

dam floated and the lake burst around the dam. All the water in the lake poured out. A wall of water 2,000 feet (600 meters) high flooded eastern Washington, carving deep channels across the land.

After the flood, the ice dam blocked the rivers again, and another lake formed. Scientists believe there were twenty-five to forty floods over a period of several thousand years. These huge floods scraped all the soil from the channels they flooded, leaving behind bare rock. Scientists do not know exactly how long it took for the river and land to recover from the floods. The walls of the deep canyons still show the scars where boulders and trees carried by the floods scraped the rock.

The streams in much of eastern Washington flow through the deep canyons carved by the floods. The Willamette Valley in Oregon has rocks carried hundreds of miles from northern Idaho by these ancient floods.

THE COLUMBIA RIVER BASIN

The area that supplies water to a particular stream or river is called a watershed. A watershed is like a giant basin, and the Columbia River watershed is known as the Columbia River Basin. A ridge, hilltop, or mountaintop divides one watershed from the next. Rain and snow that fall on one side of the ridge travel downhill to a river in that watershed. Rain and snow on the other side fall into a different watershed and end up in a different river. A watershed catches and stores water under the ground and slowly releases the water, called groundwater, into streams and rivers. If the ground cannot store any more water, water will flow on the ground as runoff and eventually end up in streams and rivers. All the water in the Columbia River Basin eventually flows into the Columbia River, and the Columbia carries the water to the ocean.

Watersheds are different sizes. The Columbia River Basin is the biggest watershed in the Pacific Northwest. It covers 258,000 square miles (668,000 square kilometers) and includes part of Canada's province of British Columbia; most of Washington, Oregon, and Idaho; and smaller parts of Montana, Wyoming, and Nevada. The watershed of a stream might be small, including just a single valley. Hundreds of streams and rivers flow into the Columbia

River, and the Columbia River Basin includes all of these smaller watersheds.

Mountain ranges circle most of the Columbia River Basin. The eastern edge of this huge watershed runs along the peaks of the Rocky Mountains in Canada and Montana. The western edge of the basin runs along the ridges of the Cascade Mountains in Washington and the Coast Ranges in Oregon.

WHAT MAKES THE COLUMBIA RIVER AN ECOSYSTEM?

The Columbia River is an aquatic, or water-based, ecosystem. Many plants and animals in this kind of ecosystem live in the water. An aquatic ecosystem also includes the land close to the river, called the riparian area. Although the plants and animals in the riparian area do not have to live in the water, they need to live near the rivers and streams to survive. Trees such as cottonwoods and willows grow in riparian areas, where the water supply is near the surface of the ground. They cannot survive in an area where the water supply is deep below the surface.

The Columbia River ecosystem includes the Columbia River and all of its tributaries, the smaller streams or rivers that flow into a

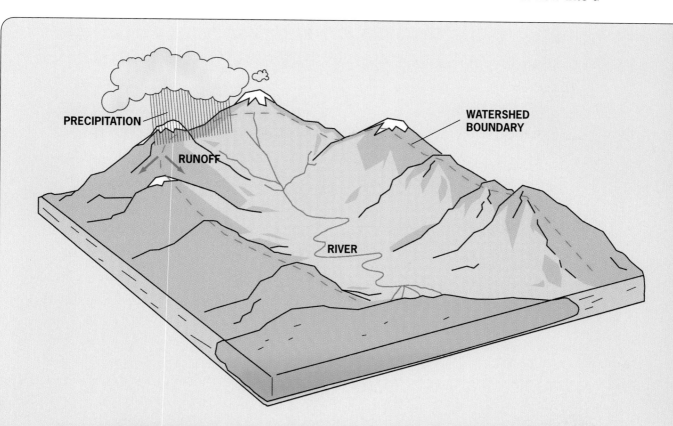

A WATERSHED IS THE AREA THAT SUPPLIES WATER TO A PARTICULAR STREAM OR RIVER.

larger river. The ecosystem includes all of the watershed's streams that flow down the watershed's mountains, the mid-sized rivers that the streams flow into, the large rivers (the Columbia and the Snake) that they flow into, and all of the riparian areas that border these streams and rivers.

Like other ecosystems, the Columbia River ecosystem has a community of plants and animals, and a nonliving environment— soil, rocks, and the water itself. The Columbia River ecosystem has the three elements found in any ecosystem. It has structures, including deep pools and side channels. It has functions, including spawning (reproducing) and log decay. And it has composition, including species of trout and beavers.

While an aquatic ecosystem like the Columbia River ecosystem is different from terrestrial, or land-based, ecosystems, the two are closely connected. The river flows through many different ecosystems on its way to the ocean, and they are all part of the Columbia River Basin.

A river's headwaters are the place where the river begins. At the Columbia's headwaters in the Rocky Mountains, the winters are cold with lots of snow, and the

(NEAR RIGHT) **COTTONWOOD TREES GROWING ALONG THE SNAKE RIVER, EAST OF RIRIE, IDAHO**

(CENTER) **MIXED DECIDUOUS AND CONIFEROUS FOREST ALONG THE ILLECILLEWAET RIVER, A TRIBUTARY OF THE COLUMBIA, IN GLACIER NATIONAL PARK, BRITISH COLUMBIA**

(FAR RIGHT) **VANTAGE CANYON IN THE COLUMBIA RIVER PLATEAU, WASHINGTON**

summers are dry. The ecosystem here is the pine and fir forest of the Rocky Mountains. After leaving the Rockies, the Columbia River flows through eastern Washington, an area that has cold, dry winters and hot, dry summers. There are fewer mountains but lots of plateaus divided by deep canyons. Because the climate and landscape are different from the Rocky Mountains, the ecosystem is different too. The ecosystem of the Columbia River Plateau is dominated by sagebrush and wild grasses, because there is not enough water for trees to grow.

Different animals live here than live in the pine forest of the mountains.

Still farther downriver, the Columbia River flows through the Cascades and then through western Oregon and Washington. Here the winters are mild and wet, with lots of rain and snow, and the summers are warm and dry. The climate is once again wet enough for trees to grow. But because the climate is warmer and wetter than in the Rocky Mountains, a different kind of forest grows. Here the forest is dominated by Douglas firs and hemlocks.

CHAPTER 2

IN THE MOUNTAINS:
STREAMS

Where does the water that flows in the Columbia River come from? Though the headwaters of the Columbia River are Columbia Lake, in the Canadian Rockies, the Columbia actually begins in many places. The river begins in all the mountain ranges of the Columbia River Basin—the Rockies, the Bitterroots, the Cascades, and others. It begins with the snow that falls on these mountains in the winter—sometimes as much as 20 feet (6 meters) in a single winter. When the snow begins to melt in the spring, water trickles through mountain meadows and pine forests.

The river also begins with the rain falling throughout the Columbia River Basin. Rain falls on the mountains, forests, farms, and cities on the land surrounding the river. Raindrops drip off the trees, fall to the ground, and soak into the soil. Water moves through the air spaces between the particles of soil. Some water is absorbed by roots, and then travels up a blade of grass or up a tree to the leaves. Some of the water evaporates into the air. The

MELTING SNOW FEEDING THE UPPER NORTH SANTIAM RIVER, OREGON

rest of the water moves slowly down through the ground, pulled by gravity.

The water moving through the air spaces in the soil is called groundwater. There is a tremendous amount of water underneath the ground, beneath the trees and other plants, moving slowly downhill throughout the Columbia River Basin. The top of the groundwater layer is called the water table. The water table can be anywhere from very deep underground to right at the surface. The level of the water table depends on how much rain and snow fall in the area and on the type of soil and rock in the area.

In places where a channel cuts into the ground, the groundwater reaches the surface of the earth, drains out into the channel, and creates a small stream. Groundwater and surface water are actually the same water. The terms describe only where the water is at any particular moment.

If all of the air spaces in the ground fill up with water, the ground cannot hold any more. Then the rest of the water, the runoff, travels downhill along the surface of the ground and into streams. As it flows over the ground, the runoff carries sediment—soil, leaves, and sometimes rocks—into the streams.

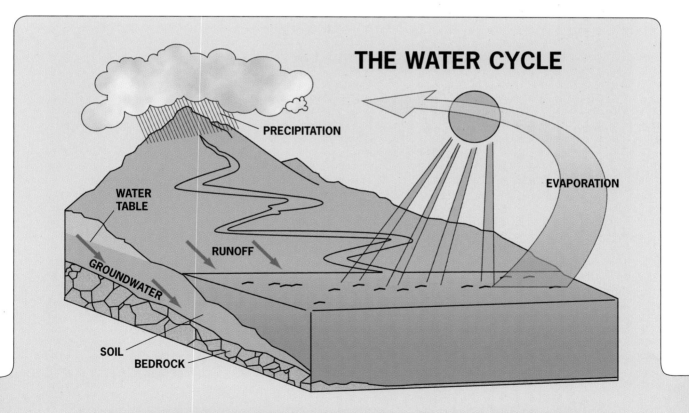

THE WATER CYCLE

PRECIPITATION

EVAPORATION

WATER TABLE

RUNOFF

GROUNDWATER

SOIL

BEDROCK

WATER EVAPORATING FROM THE GROUND, FROM BODIES OF WATER, AND FROM THE LEAVES OF PLANTS FORMS INTO CLOUDS THAT START THE WATER CYCLE ALL OVER AGAIN.

Small streams flow downhill through mountain valleys. The valleys are V-shaped—very narrow at the bottom, with steep sides. The streams flow straight along the bottom of the narrow "V", dropping quickly down the steep mountainsides. As the running streams merge, and as more and more water comes in from the groundwater, the streams gradually get bigger.

Steps and pools are the main structures of small streams. Streams have a series of small pools, with short drops or steps between the pools. From the side, the streams look almost like a flight of stairs, with water cascading down the steps. The pools provide habitat for fish and other organisms.

The steps are formed by boulders, or by trees that have fallen into streams from the riparian areas. The steps may be short waterfalls or gentle drops. Whatever shape they take, the steps allow the water to drop quickly without eroding all the soil beneath it. When water falls over a step, it

A SERIES OF POOLS CAUSED BY TREES FALLING ACROSS A STREAM

digs out a pool below. The pools slow the water down. The steps and pools soften the water's force and limit the amount of erosion it causes. If the water plunged straight down the mountainside, it would cut deeply into the soil. But the water only drops a short distance over each step, and then is caught in the pool below the step.

The bottom of each pool is covered with small stones called gravel. Some water sinks down through the gravel into the groundwater, but most of the water stays in the stream.

The steps and pools are especially important when it rains hard and when the winter snow melts in the spring. During these times, the ground can't absorb all the water, and the excess becomes runoff. Runoff swells the streams, and they run much higher for a few days. If the streams didn't have the steps and pools, the water would deeply erode the soil.

In small mountain streams, trees that have fallen from riparian areas may stretch across the entire stream. Some of these logs pile up against each other, forming groups of logs called logjams. Logjams form an important part of the stream structure. Besides forming steps and pools, they provide habitat for many animals, including larvae. Larvae are insects in early stages of their development, after they have hatched and before they change into their adult forms. They find homes on the rough surfaces of the wood. And fish find hiding places in the water under the logs.

The larvae and other life-forms living in the streams require a supply of energy.

STREAMS HAVE A SERIES OF SMALL POOLS, WITH SHORT DROPS OR STEPS BETWEEN THE POOLS. FROM THE SIDE, THE STREAMS LOOK ALMOST LIKE A FLIGHT OF STAIRS, WITH WATER CASCADING DOWN THE STEPS.

PRIMARY CONSUMERS: AQUATIC INSECT LARVAE

All insect species lay eggs. Some species drop their eggs into water, or they lay their eggs on leaves or plant stems overhanging the water. Insect eggs hatch into larvae, an early stage of life. Aquatic larvae live in water—they breathe through gills and are able to take oxygen from the water. Larvae need lots of oxygen, and they depend on the constant flow of water in streams and rivers to supply it. Hundreds of different species of aquatic larvae live in the streams and rivers of the Columbia Basin.

After these larvae spend one to three years living in the water, they grow into adult insects that have wings and can fly. The winged adults may live only a few days or even only a few hours. Big swarms of insects fly near the streams, usually on summer days and evenings. The adult insects mate and lay eggs, and the life cycle of their species begins again. In Columbia Basin streams, three of the most important groups of aquatic insects are caddisflies, mayflies, and stoneflies.

Most **caddisfly** (*Trichoptera*) larvae build small cases from tiny stones, sticks, pieces of leaves, or grains of sand to protect themselves. They drag these cases as they crawl around the stream bottom and can pull inside when they sense danger. Then their cases look like they are just sticks or stones on the stream bottom. These caddisfly larvae graze algae from the surfaces of stones or wood, or they eat plant material in the

**CADDISFLY LARVAE ON STONES
AT THE BOTTOM OF A STREAM**

water. Other species of caddisfly larvae build tiny, silky nets. Their nets filter algae from the water, and the caddisfly larvae eat the algae.

There are many species of **mayflies** (*Ephemeroptera*) and they have many different shapes. All mayfly species have three tail-like strands at the end of their bodies. Mayfly larvae graze on algae, filter algae from the water current, or graze on plant material fallen into the water.

Stonefly (*Plecoptera*) larvae are usually bigger than mayfly larvae. They have two tail-like filaments at the end of their abdomens.

MAYFLY PERCHED ON HAIRCAP MOSS (*POLYTRICHUM*)

Aquatic insect larvae are primary consumers. They consume algae and plant material in streams and rivers. The hundreds of different species have many different ways of eating algae and plants. Some larvae graze on algae attached to rocks, others eat algae drifting in the water, and others shred wood and leaves into smaller particles that they can eat. Aquatic insect larvae are known as grazers, shredders, scrapers, or collectors, depending on how they get their food. Larvae are eaten by larger insects and are a main food source for fish.

In small mountain streams, the energy supply comes mostly from the trees and other plants in the riparian areas next to the streams. The trees and plants drop leaves and needles into the stream, and eventually the trees die and fall into the streams. All this plant material provides a source of food for living creatures in the stream, including snails, clams, aquatic larvae, and many other small animals.

Since the mountain streams of the Columbia River Basin usually run through forests of pine, fir, and cedar trees, the water is shaded by the trees. Very little sunlight reaches the water, so not many plants can live in these streams. Only algae—simple organisms that live in water or moist soil—can grow in these streams, and they grow only in small quantities.

As streams get larger, the forest does not shade the entire stream. More sunlight reaches the water, and more algae grow there than can grow in small streams. Algae are an important food source in these streams.

In addition to providing structure and habitat, logs that fall into streams are a food source. As the wood absorbs water, fungi begin to decay, or break down, the wood. This process makes the wood softer and easier for larvae to eat. Fungi are plants such as mushrooms and molds that cannot get energy from the sun like algae can. Since fungi cannot make their own food, they feed on dead plants and animals. Snails scrape the wood surfaces

HAIRY PARCHMENT FUNGUS
(STEREUM HIRSUTUM)

to get food. As logs are scraped and eaten, they develop rough surfaces that provide homes for more organisms.

Fungi continue to grow deeper into the logs. The logs are so large that they take many years to decay. They provide a long-lasting source of food.

The snails and larvae that eat plant matter are in turn eaten by fish and salamanders. The most common fish in mountain streams is the cutthroat trout, named after the red stripe on its throat.

A mammal species that lives in streams (and rivers) is the beaver. Beavers are dark brown, medium-sized mammals that grow to be up to 46 inches (120 centimeters) long. They have large, flat, paddle-shaped tails. They build dams from trees, branches, and mud. Beaver dams can help add to the structure of small streams. Beavers cut down trees in order to get at their food, the tender bark on the branches. They fell trees by chewing through the trunks with their long front teeth. Then they strip the bark from

BEAVER *(CASTOR CANADENSIS)* REPAIRING A DAM

the branches, eat it, and drop the peeled branches into the water. Beavers build underground dens in the riverbank, complete with underwater entrances.

When animals die, they become a source of energy for the ecosystem. Through the process of decay, fungi, bacteria, and some species of animals eat and process dead animal matter. As the matter decays, it provides food for other living organisms, and so energy is recycled back into the ecosystem. Death and decay are important functions in an ecosystem, just as birth, growth, and reproduction are important functions.

The structures of the stream ecosystem are constantly changing. Some changes happen slowly—such as logs decaying in the water—and are hard to notice. Other changes, such as landslides, happen quickly and have dramatic results.

Landslides don't happen very often in the same place, but they are a normal event in the steep mountain ranges of the Columbia River Basin. Landslides usually happen in places where some or all of the trees are gone and there are no tree roots to hold the soil in place. They are most likely to happen when very heavy rains fall over several days. When a landslide occurs, all the soil, rocks, and trees on a mountainside slide down into one of the narrow valleys. Large landslides can scrape away everything in their path, carrying it all downhill. Although landslides can do a lot of damage to a stream, they also supply logs, boulders, and sediment—the materials that give streams structure.

As small streams come down from the mountains, they meet other streams and join, forming larger streams. The narrow valleys of the mountains become wider. The mountain streams supply cold, clear water and materials that will provide structure and energy to the rivers they flow into.

CHAPTER 3

COMING OUT OF THE MOUNTAINS:
MEDIUM-SIZED RIVERS

When does a stream become a river? There is no exact moment, no certain size a stream must be, when this happens. But as streams get larger, they are called rivers. The Okanogan, Wenatchee, John Day, and McKenzie are some of the medium-sized rivers in the Columbia River Basin.

Rivers are not just wider and deeper than streams—they have different and more complex structures than streams. A river has pools, but they are much deeper and larger than the pools in streams. Instead of steps or waterfalls between pools, rivers have riffles, or stretches of choppy, fast-moving water. Some riffles develop into rapids with white-capped waves, also known as whitewater.

River valleys are usually wider than the V-shaped mountain valleys, so the water is no longer forced to follow a straight path. The rivers meander—they wander back and forth across the valley in big, loopy curves. As rivers meander across their wide, flat valleys, they form gravel bars and side

THE NORTH FORK OF THE JOHN DAY RIVER, OREGON

channels. Gravel bars are long, flat areas of gravel that just barely rise above the river's normal water level. Side channels cut around the far side of islands and some gravel bars. The current is usually slower in the side channels.

River valleys also have terraces—slightly raised areas of land alongside the river. Terraces are usually flat on top, but often have steep banks that slope down to the river.

Logjams and driftwood logs are important structures in rivers. Rivers get many of their logs from mountain streams. During floods, whole trees and large branches are carried downstream by the powerful current. The driftwood logs float into logjams, where they are held by the other logs already there. Floods also topple other trees into the river from its banks, adding to the driftwood logs in the water.

Logjams help to create a river's pools, riffles, meanders, and side channels. Large logjams may build along a side channel, or at the upstream end of a gravel bar or island. The logs slow down the river's current or change its direction. Water may flow around a big logjam, leaving a quiet side channel behind the logs. Or water may pour over a driftwood log and scour a pool on the log's downstream side. The river affects the logs too—the current moves driftwood logs into new patterns every time the water is high from rain and runoff.

While logjams can slow down the river's current or change its direction, they do not block the river completely, the way a dam does. Some water flows underneath and between the logs, so fish and other aquatic animals can travel through the logjams. Logjams do block

> WHILE LOGJAMS CAN SLOW DOWN THE RIVER'S CURRENT OR CHANGE ITS DIRECTION, THEY DO NOT BLOCK THE RIVER COMPLETELY, THE WAY A DAM DOES. SOME WATER FLOWS UNDERNEATH AND BETWEEN THE LOGS.

many leaves, needles, and branches from floating downstream, however. They hold this plant material in one place, giving the fungi, larvae, and snails time to eat and digest it.

When rivers flood, the receding water leaves behind floodplains—flat areas covered with sediment. These areas may be covered by floodwaters again and again, year after year. The river reworks the floodplains, changing its channels with every flood.

What causes floods? In the valleys of the Columbia River Basin, most rain falls in the winter. Rivers run higher as water from the winter rain pours into them. While the valleys are getting rain, the mountain ranges are getting lots of snow. But if the weather turns warm and rain falls on the snow, melting it early, the combination of rain and melting snow causes a winter flood. When the snow melts in the spring, it creates spring runoff. If heavy rains fall during spring runoff, the extra water causes spring floods.

Healthy riparian areas have many trees, bushes, and other plants. The roots of these plants help to hold the riverbanks in place, so the water constantly flowing by does not erode the banks. But floods tear out some trees and bushes—roots and all—and carry them downriver until they are caught in logjams or against rocks. Trees and other plants begin to grow back between floods.

Since floods wash over different areas in different years, patches of older forest grow near patches of younger forest in riparian areas. The age of the trees is sometimes a clue as to how long it has been since the last flood reached a particular spot. Terraces often have older forests because only the biggest floods are high enough to pour over terraces. And even when floodwater does reach the older, bigger trees on a terrace, they aren't always torn out, because big trees have more extensive root systems than small trees.

Riparian areas act like giant sponges. During floods, water soaks into these areas. Healthy riparian areas can store large amounts of water. Some of this water becomes groundwater. Riparian areas help to filter sediments, including some types of pollution, out of the groundwater. In late summer, when little rain falls and the rivers are low, riparian areas release the stored groundwater back into the river.

The many structures of rivers create many different habitats in the water and the riparian areas. When there are more habitats, more species are found. An ecosystem with many different species of living organisms has a high level of biodiversity. Rivers usually have more biodiversity than mountain streams.

In rivers, as in streams, the energy supply for the food chain comes from both the land and the water. But rivers produce more of their own food energy than mountain streams do. Rivers are much wider than mountain streams, and trees shade only the edges of the water. More sunlight reaches the water, so more algae grow. Some algae live on rocks on the riverbed, and other types of algae float in the river current.

The trees and other plants in the riparian areas are still an important source of energy, however. Leaves, branches, and trees fall into the water and become food for larvae and other animals.

Rivers have another source of energy: the pieces of wood and plants that are constantly being carried downstream from the rivers' tributary streams. All of this plant material is eaten by the larvae living in rivers. Rivers have a greater variety and number of insect species than mountain streams do. Stonefly, mayfly, and caddisfly larvae, and larvae of other species, all live in the river.

Often, all the larvae of a particular species change to adults and emerge from the river within a few hours of each other. When this happens, large numbers of the insects fly near the river. The adult insects live only for a few days, but they are still an important part of the food chain. Birds and bats eat many of the insects. Fish jump from the water to catch insects near the water's surface.

The rivers of the Columbia River Basin have more species of snails and clams, which belong to the group of animals called mollusks, than small streams do. Although mollusks have no legs, the underside of their bodies is a large, muscular foot, with which they can move slowly.

PRIMARY PRODUCERS: ALGAE AND DIATOMS

Algae are simple living organisms that carry on photosynthesis—the process by which green plants take sunlight and use it as an energy source to change carbon dioxide and water to food. Many algae are single-celled organisms or groups of drifting cells. These tiny life-forms usually float in the water and are carried by the current. Many species of algae live in Columbia Basin streams. Diatoms are one-celled algae that have cell walls shaped in distinctive patterns.

Some species of algae form long strands that look like long, green strings. Algae do not have true stems, roots, or leaves. They don't need stems because the water supports their long strands. They don't need roots because the entire organism is always soaked in water. Some algae attach themselves to rocks, but these attachments are not true roots, because they do not absorb water. Other species of algae grow in films over the surfaces of rocks and wood on the streambed. Many algae species are green or blue-green, but some are brown or golden colored.

ALGAE IN STRING LAKE, GRAND TETON NATIONAL PARK, WYOMING

Algae are primary producers. Many different kinds of animals eat algae, including snails, aquatic larvae, and some species of fish.

Aquatic snails graze the algae that grow on rocks or eat away at the surfaces of wood that has fallen into the water. Many kinds of mollusks, such as clams, rarely move at all. Instead, they fasten themselves to a rock and filter small particles of food out of the water that flows past them.

The western pearlshell is a freshwater clam that is found in the rivers of the Columbia River Basin. This clam was once common on the rocky bottoms of streams and rivers but is now rare. Scientists have learned that the young pearlshell clams, which do not yet have shells, live for a few weeks on the gills of river fish such as trout and salmon. The young clams depend on the fish for survival. There are fewer fish in the rivers than there were years ago, so many of the young clams die.

Rivers also have a greater diversity of fish species than smaller streams, because rivers have a greater variety of habitats and a larger food supply. The fish feed on the many insects and on some of the mollusks, such as snails. Some species of fish feed on smaller fish.

River fish need the river's complex structures to live. They need logjams and deep pools to provide food and cover for them. Fish need hiding places because many animals, including bald eagles, ospreys, and river otters, eat fish. Small fish need to hide from larger fish. Fish also need safe places in side channels and among logjams, where the current is slower, so that during floods they can keep from being washed downstream by the powerful current.

Different species of fish use different habitats for spawning, or reproducing. Fish spawn when the female releases eggs into the water, and the male releases milt over the eggs to fertilize them.

Rainbow trout and bull trout are two species of fish that live in the rivers of the Columbia River Basin. Rainbow trout originally lived in the streams and rivers of the Pacific Coast, from Alaska to southern California. During the twentieth century, some rainbow trout were transplanted into Rocky Mountain streams, and the species can be found in some inland western streams as well. Rainbow trout can grow to be more than 3 feet (1 meter) long, although they usually grow to only about 1 foot (0.3 meter). They have black spots on their backs and sides, and a red, rainbow-like band down their sides. These trout feed mainly on insects.

Bull trout are not as widespread as rainbow trout. Bull trout can only live in the very coldest, cleanest rivers, and are found in only a few rivers in the Columbia River Basin. Bull trout eat smaller fish.

Salmon are also found in many rivers of the Columbia River Basin. Unlike trout, salmon do not spend their entire lives in freshwater rivers. Salmon are anadromous fish—they hatch in freshwater, migrate to the ocean where they grow to be adults, and then return to streams and rivers to spawn.

Many birds and other animals are also part of the Columbia River ecosystem. They live in the riparian areas along rivers, and they depend on the river for their food.

Two of the largest birds in the ecosystem are ospreys and eagles. Bald eagles grow to be up to 43 inches (110 centimeters) long. Their wingspan can be more than 7 feet (2 meters) across. They have brownish black bodies and white-feathered heads. Eagles build large nests in tall trees, usually partway down the tree. Bald eagles eat living or dead fish, and they also hunt birds such as ducks.

Ospreys can be up to 24 inches (61 centimeters) long. They have dark brown backs, with white heads and white chests. Ospreys eat only fish that they hunted. They catch fish by plunging into the water, feet first, and scooping up a fish in their strong, sharp claws, called talons. Ospreys build large nests on the tops of tall trees, always very close to the water. They will often choose a tree whose top has broken off, providing a platform for the nest. Ospreys have a loud, high-pitched cry.

Many species of smaller birds also live in the riparian area. One of these species, the dipper, is a plain gray bird that is slightly smaller than a robin. Dippers can often be seen standing on a rock at the water's edge, bobbing up and down. Suddenly, the dipper will fly right into the water.

(LEFT) **OSPREYS** *(PANDION HALIAETUS)* **IN THEIR NEST**

(BELOW) **AMERICAN DIPPER** *(CINCLUS MEXICANUS)*

(RIGHT) **RIVER OTTER** *(LUTRA CANADENSIS)*

Underwater, the dipper will run along the river bottom with its wings half-open, searching for aquatic insects. Dippers build their nests out of moss, on a rock cliff by the river's edge or hidden among tree roots on the bank. The dipper's song sounds like the river itself—it is a loud, rapid, bubbling sound, much like the sound of fast-flowing riffles.

Two of the many mammal species that live in the riparian areas are beavers, who live in streams too, and river otters. Both of these animals spend much of their time in the river.

River otters are dark brown, medium-sized mammals that grow to be up to 51 inches (130 centimeters) long. They have long bodies with long tails and can swim very fast underwater. They mostly hunt and eat fish, but sometimes they hunt small animals on land too. Otters usually dig their dens in forested riparian areas, often right along riverbanks. Otters love to play. They make their own waterslides on muddy or snowy riverbanks and slide into the water over and over again.

CHAPTER 4
IN THE VALLEYS:
LARGE RIVERS

Large rivers have the same basic structures as mid-sized rivers—pools, riffles, logjams, meanders, gravel bars, and side channels. But large rivers are wider and deeper than mid-sized rivers. They have wider valleys, and they meander across wide floodplains. Also, a large river's side channels are often braided—many side channels loop back into the main channel. Some large rivers in the Columbia River Basin are the Snake River and the Willamette River. They are tributaries of the Columbia River, which is the largest river in the watershed.

Large rivers have much larger riparian areas than smaller rivers—the riparian areas reach out to the edges of their wide

JOHN DAY RIVER, OREGON

floodplains. These riparian areas include islands, wetlands, terraces, and floodplains. The wide floodplains of large rivers have old and young riparian forests. And large rivers have driftwood logs from past floods.

The logjams in large rivers are themselves large and provide important structure. They hold leaves and wood in the river, providing food chain sources. The large logjams affect the river current—they slow down the water or change its direction of flow, which helps to create pools, gravel bars, islands, and side channels (including braided channels). The logs themselves slowly decay, and so they, too, are a part of the food chain.

Riparian forests are important to large rivers. The trees shade the water along the edges of the river, keeping the water cooler. The trees also protect the riverbanks from erosion and provide habitat for many riparian species, and they eventually fall in the river and become driftwood.

In a large river, the food chain has three sources: algae, bits of plant material from upstream, and plant material from the floodplains. Large rivers are deeper than mid-sized rivers, and the water is not as clear. Very little sunlight reaches the river bottom, so algae can't live there. Instead, the algae in large rivers float in the upper part of the water, where sunlight can reach them.

The plant material carried downstream by the current has been shredded into tiny pieces by aquatic larvae and other animals upstream. Some species of larvae and mollusks that live in large rivers are able to filter these tiny pieces of plant material from the water and collect them for food.

> **RIPARIAN FORESTS ARE IMPORTANT TO LARGE RIVERS. THE TREES SHADE THE WATER ALONG THE EDGES OF THE RIVER, KEEPING THE WATER COOLER. THE TREES ALSO PROTECT THE RIVERBANKS FROM EROSION.**

TOP-LEVEL CONSUMER: BALD EAGLE
(Haliaeetus leucocephalus)

Adult bald eagles grow to be up to 43 inches (110 centimeters) long, measured from the tip of their beak to the tip of their tail. Their wingspans can be more than 7 feet (2 meters) across. Adult bald eagles have snow-white heads, necks, and tails. They have a hooked yellow beak and big, strong talons. The rest of their body is brownish black. Young eagles—up to five years old—have brown heads.

Bald eagles usually live near large rivers and lakes or on seacoasts. Eagles build large nests in tall trees, usually part of the way down a tree. They add sticks to the same nest every year. Female eagles lay one to three eggs.

Bald eagles are secondary consumers. They are at the top of the food chain with just a few other animals, including otters. Bald eagles have no predators.

Bald eagles eat living or dead fish. They like to eat adult salmon that have spawned, died, and washed up on the riverbanks. Eagles can catch fish in shallow water, and sometimes they even steal fish caught by other birds such as osprey. Bald eagles also catch and eat ducks.

Plant materials from the riparian areas and floodplains, such as logs, sticks, and leaves, also provide sources of food. Large quantities of these plant materials are carried into the river during floods.

With their many side channels, pools, wetlands, and logjams, large rivers offer a wide diversity of habitats. They have many of the same species found in mid-sized rivers, such as rainbow trout, river otters, and bald eagles, plus many others.

Large rivers are home to large fish. The largest fish in the Columbia River is the white sturgeon. This fish can be more than 12 feet (3.7 meters) long and weigh more than 1,200 pounds (540 kilograms). It has bony plates instead of scales and looks slightly like a shark, although the two are not related. Sturgeon eat smaller fish and mollusks. White sturgeon can live to be one hundred years old.

Young salmon are part of the food chain as they pass through large rivers on their way downstream to the ocean. Northern pikeminnow, other kinds of fish, and other animals feed on the young salmon.

Adult salmon swim up large rivers when they are returning to freshwater to spawn.

The returning salmon do not eat after they leave the ocean, but they are an important part of the food chain. Many predators eat the returning salmon. Black bears catch salmon as they swim upstream. Sometimes bald eagles gather in large numbers by rivers where salmon are swimming upstream in order to feast on them. Seals and sea lions travel up the estuary of the lower Columbia River to feed on the migrating salmon. Smaller animals, such as deer mice and raccoons, feed off dead fish after their bodies wash up on shore.

Other kinds of anadromous fish besides salmon, including steelhead, sea-run cutthroat trout, American shad, and Pacific lamprey, live in large rivers in the Columbia River Basin. The Pacific lamprey is a long, slender fish that is shaped like an eel and grows up to 30 inches (80 centimeters) long. In the ocean, the lamprey attaches to the bodies of other fish, piercing a hole in their bodies, and sucks their blood. The lamprey feeds off the fish without sucking enough blood to kill them. Like salmon, the lamprey does not feed once it returns to freshwater to spawn.

Many kinds of birds live in the riparian areas of large rivers. Some species, like the great blue heron, are predators that feed on fish and other aquatic animals. The great blue heron is a tall bird that is up to 48 inches (120 centimeters) from head to tail. These birds hunt for fish, frogs, and other animals in wetlands and along riverbanks. Often, many great blue herons build their nests near each other—sometimes several pairs nest in the same tree.

The Canada goose is another large bird, up to 45 inches (110 centimeters) from head to tail. These long-necked birds are dark, with some white on their throat and belly. Geese have long necks and wide bills for eating plants. Canada geese nest in riparian areas—in marshes, along low islands, or on banks along lakes and rivers. They build their nests on the ground, hidden among plants.

Many species of ducks live in the Columbia River Basin. Ducks eat mostly aquatic plants, but they sometimes eat snails

LAMPREY (LAMPETRA AYRESI) ON CARP (CYPRINUS) HOST. (CARP ARE NOT NATIVE TO THE COLUMBIA BASIN—THEY WERE INTRODUCED BY HUMANS.)

GREAT BLUE HERON (ARDEA HERODIAS) WITH ITS CATCH

and other small aquatic animals. Various duck species gather in large numbers on the reservoirs, lakes, and wetlands of the Columbia River Basin over the winter. Some of these ducks stay in the Columbia River Basin all year, while others fly north in the summer.

Change is important in large rivers, just as it is in streams and mid-sized rivers. Floods are the main large-scale change in large rivers. Rivers often run high and have minor flooding during the winter and spring. Major floods happen only occasionally.

Major floods don't happen very often, but they are crucial for river ecosystems.

Floods renew river ecosystems and help to create the complex structures and diverse habitats of large rivers. When a large river floods, water flows over the riverbanks and across large parts of the floodplain. The surging water cuts new side channels and changes the shape of old ones. Some of the floodwater soaks into the riparian area and wetlands, and becomes part of the groundwater. Logs, sticks, leaves, and plants are washed away and carried into the river. After a flood, there is often a burst of new life in the river, because the material washed into the river is a major source of food energy for the river ecosystem.

CHAPTER 5

WILD SALMON:
A KEYSTONE SPECIES

Wild salmon are keystone species in the Columbia River ecosystem. A keystone species is a central element in an ecosystem. Wild salmon play a central role in the food chain. Their presence or absence affects the health of the entire ecosystem. Salmon travel thousands of miles in their lifetimes and face many dangers and difficulties in returning to their home streams to spawn.

THE SALMON LIFE CYCLE

The life cycle of the wild salmon begins and ends in freshwater streams, lakes, and rivers. Salmon are anadromous fish—they hatch in freshwater, migrate to the ocean where they grow to be adults, and then return to freshwater to spawn. Adult salmon return to their home stream—the same stream in which they were born.

A salmon begins its life as an egg deposited in the gravel of a stream or lake. Two large, dark eyes are the first sign of the young salmon growing in the egg. Fish biologists say that the eggs are "eyed up" at this stage.

When the salmon hatches from its egg, it is called an alevin. It still has a yellowish orange yolk sac attached to its body. The

SALMON EGGS

SALMON ALEVIN WITH YOLK SAC

alevin hides in the gravel of the streambed for several weeks, getting all of its food from the yolk sac. When the yolk is gone, the salmon swims out of the gravel and into the stream. At this stage, the salmon is called a fry.

Salmon fry live in freshwater, eating aquatic larvae and other small organisms. Salmon fry need clean, cold water, lots of food, and places where they are protected from floods and where they can hide from predators. Their bodies have dark brown and black spots and bands that camouflage the fish and help them hide from predators.

At a certain point, the fry are ready to migrate to the ocean. Then they are called smolts. The point at which they migrate varies for different species of salmon. Some migrate to the ocean a few weeks after they are born, while others spend one, two, or three years in freshwater before they head for the ocean.

The smolts must change in many ways so that they can live in saltwater instead of in freshwater. For example, their bodies need to be able to get rid of excess salt. The smolts become a solid silver color, and they become slimmer. Smolts let the current carry them downstream from their home stream or river to the Columbia River, then down the Columbia to the estuary at the river's mouth. Salmon smolts spend some time in the mixed saltwater and freshwater of the estuary, eating the rich supplies of food—many kinds of shrimplike animals, insect larvae and adults, and small fish such as young herring.

When they are ready, the smolts swim out into the Pacific Ocean. Salmon spend most of their adult life—from one to five

COHO SALMON (ONCORHYNCHUS KISUTCH) FRY

ADULT CHINOOK SALMON (ONCORHYNCHUS TSHAWYTSCHA)

years—in the ocean, swimming thousands of miles. They eat smaller fish and grow in size. In the ocean, large fish, such as tuna, and marine mammals, such as seals and dolphins, eat the salmon. When adult salmon are ready to spawn, they begin to migrate back to their home stream. Salmon may travel hundreds of miles in their journey home.

The adult salmon's bodies change when they return to freshwater, as they prepare to spawn and die. The male's upper jaw develops into a long, hooked snout. The hook curves down toward his mouth. Male sockeye and pink salmon grow large humps on their backs. Male and female sockeye salmon change color. Their backs turn bright red and their heads turn olive green. Chum salmon get purple, pink, and yellow streaks on their sides. Chinook turn almost black after they return to freshwater. Coho males change color to having green backs and dull red sides.

Scientists do not completely understand how salmon are able to find their way from the open ocean back to the place where they hatched. But from wherever they are in the ocean, the salmon know exactly where they have to go and when they need to leave in order to get there at the same time as others born in their home stream. Fish biologists have tagged salmon to learn more about where they travel. The biologists have found that salmon from a particular river do not stay together in the ocean, but range widely over the North Pacific.

Scientists believe salmon have some sort of internal compass that enables them to detect changes in the earth's magnetic field, using this to find their

> SCIENTISTS DO NOT COMPLETELY UNDERSTAND HOW SALMON ARE ABLE TO FIND THEIR WAY FROM THE OPEN OCEAN BACK TO THE PLACE WHERE THEY HATCHED.

way. They may also use the position of the sun in the sky as a clue. The fish are also able to tell the difference between their home river and nearby rivers. Once they reach the area near their home river, salmon may start to travel up several different rivers. They are able to tell when they are swimming up the wrong river. Salmon may use their highly developed sense of smell to detect the scent of the stream where they hatched.

When something has damaged their home stream, the salmon swim to a nearby stream to spawn instead. For example, in 1980 the volcanic eruption of Mount Saint Helens in Washington filled the Toutle River with mud and ashes. When the salmon returned that year, they turned away from the Toutle River and spawned in the nearby Kalama River instead.

As they enter the river, salmon swim upriver against the current. They are strong and can fight their way upriver through powerful currents and rapids. Salmon can leap past waterfalls 10 or more feet (over 3 meters) high, and they continue to swim upstream through the strong currents at the

MIGRATING SOCKEYE SALMON (ONCORHYNCHUS NERKA) JUMPING A WATERFALL

top of the waterfalls. The salmon do not eat after they leave the ocean and return to freshwater.

When adult salmon reach their home streams, they spawn. The female salmon turns on her side and uses her tail to build a nest-shaped area, called a redd, in the gravel. A male salmon that has paired up with her chases other male salmon away from the redd and nips the other males if they don't leave. He swims very close to the female, staying next to her. The female lays up to several thousand eggs, dropping them over the redd. The male releases milt at the same time, and the milt fertilizes the eggs. The fertilized eggs sink down to the bottom of the redd, and the female covers them with gravel. The eggs are protected in the gravel until they hatch. The water in the streams and rivers flows through the gravel, providing oxygen to the eggs and alevins. If too much sediment settles on top of the spawning gravel, the soil may smother the eggs.

Migration, courtship, and spawning take every bit of energy that the adult salmon have. They die shortly after spawning.

The adult salmon continue to be an important part of the food chain even after they die. Many animals feed on the bodies of salmon that wash up on the riverbanks. Bald eagles, raccoons, and other animals feed on the bodies.

Many of the dead salmon decay in the water, and their dead bodies provide energy to the food chain. Their bodies provide nutrients for algae and water plants such as moss. Their bodies also feed bacteria, fungi, larvae, and other small water animals that in turn are food for the young salmon.

FEMALE SOCKEYE PREPARING A REDD AS A MALE STANDS GUARD

KEYS TO FIT THOUSANDS OF LOCKS: THE DIVERSITY OF COLUMBIA SALMON

The salmon of the Columbia River and its tributaries belong to five different species: chinook, chum, coho, sockeye, and pink salmon. Two other species of fish are closely related to salmon: steelhead and cutthroat. Each of these seven species returns to different streams, lakes, and rivers of the Columbia River Basin, and each species lives in different habitats.

Chum and pink salmon return only to the lower end of the Columbia River, to tributary rivers up as far as the Columbia Gorge. Coho salmon return to tributaries in the lower and mid-river Columbia River Basin. Chinook salmon travel as far upriver as they can in the large and medium-sized rivers but don't swim into smaller streams. Sockeye salmon also travel to the upper Columbia River Basin, but they only spawn in or near lakes. They return to rivers that have lakes at the upper end, such as Redfish Lake in Idaho and Lake Wenatchee in Washington.

Although there are only five salmon species, there are hundreds of salmon stocks. A salmon stock is a local population of a salmon species that migrates to a particular river or lake at a specific season in order to spawn. Willamette River spring chinook and Snake River fall chinook are two examples of different salmon stocks. Salmon stocks are sometimes referred to as salmon runs, because each stock "runs" up its home stream in the same time period. The salmon runs of the Columbia River Basin begin in early spring and continue through late fall.

Each salmon stock has a different life history—over many generations it has adapted to the unique conditions of its specific stream. Some stocks are better able to fight off certain diseases or adapt to different temperatures or stream flows. Different stocks spend different amounts of time in freshwater, migrate to the ocean at different seasons, and spawn at different times. Each stock uses habitats at a slightly different time of the year. Because of these different life histories, salmon stocks don't compete directly with one another for food.

SALMON OF THE COLUMBIA RIVER BASIN

Chinook Salmon *(Oncorhynchus tshawytscha)*

Chinook are the largest salmon species. They can grow up to 5 feet (more than 1 meter) long and weigh more than 100 pounds (50 kilograms), although most chinook weigh less than 50 pounds (20 kilograms). They are also known as king salmon. Chinook have migrated more than 1,200 miles (1,900 kilometers) up the river, almost to the Columbia's headwaters.

Stream-type chinook spend one or more years in freshwater and then two to four years in the ocean. The spawning adults return to freshwater in either spring or summer. Ocean-type chinook migrate to the ocean in their first year, spend two to four years in the ocean, and return to freshwater in summer and fall.

Chum Salmon

(Oncorhynchus keta)

Chum salmon are the second largest salmon species, after chinook. They can reach up to 40 inches (100 centimeters) long and 35 pounds (16 kilograms). Chum salmon are also known as dog salmon. Spawning adults develop large, sharp front teeth and patches of purple, yellow, and pink on their sides. Chum spawn in rivers in the lower Columbia River Basin.

Chum migrate to the ocean soon after hatching and spend very little time in freshwater. Chum spend two to five years in the ocean before returning to spawn.

Coho Salmon

(Oncorhynchus kisutch)

Coho are a mid-sized salmon species. Although they can weigh as much as 31 pounds (14 kilograms), coho normally weigh from 6 to 12 pounds (3 to 5 kilograms). Coho are also known as silver salmon. Coho return to streams and rivers in the lower and mid-Columbia River Basin.

Coho spend one to two years in freshwater, in small streams, before going to the ocean. During the winter, coho fry live in deep pools and side channels to keep from being washed downstream by winter floods. After one or two years in the ocean, they return to spawn.

Pink Salmon *(Oncorhynchus gorbuscha)*

Pink salmon are the smallest salmon species. Adult pinks usually weigh from 3 to 5 pounds (1 to 2 kilograms). Pink salmon are also known as humpback salmon, because mature male pinks develop large humps on their backs. Pinks return only to the lower Columbia River.

Pink salmon have a two-year life cycle. Pinks do not travel very far upriver for spawning, and the smolts migrate quickly to the ocean after hatching. Of all the salmon species, pink salmon spend the least time in freshwater.

Sockeye Salmon

(Oncorhynchus nerka)

Sockeye salmon can grow up to 33 inches (84 centimeters) long and weigh up to 15 pounds (7 kilograms), although most sockeye weigh from 4 to 8 pounds (2 to 4 kilograms). Sockeye are also called red or blueback salmon. Mature salmon returning to spawn develop green heads and bright red bodies. Like chinook, sockeye travel to the upper parts of rivers, but sockeye use only lakes or areas near lakes for spawning. Columbia River Basin sockeye travel as far as Idaho's Stanley Basin, about 900 miles (1400 kilometers) from the ocean, and Washington's Cascade Mountains.

Sockeye spawn in lakes or in rivers near lakes. The sockeye fry live in the lakes for one to three years before traveling to the ocean. Sockeye spend one to four years in the ocean before returning to spawn.

Steelhead *(Oncorhynchus mykiss)*

Steelhead are the anadromous form of rainbow trout. Until 1989 steelhead and rainbow trout were both classified as trout species. But then scientists reclassified steelhead, recognizing them as more closely related to salmon. Steelhead can grow as long as 45 inches (110 centimeters) and weigh as much as 42 pounds (19 kilograms). They have a red band on their sides. Steelhead spawn throughout the Columbia River Basin.

Steelhead spend one to four years in freshwater and one to four years in the ocean before returning to spawn in freshwater. Unlike other species of salmon, some steelhead survive spawning. They may spawn two or three times in their lifetime.

Coastal Cutthroat *(Oncorhynchus clarkii)*

Coastal, or sea-run, cutthroat are the anadromous form of cutthroat trout. Scientists reclassified cutthroat in 1989, when they realized that these fish are also closely related to salmon. Coastal cutthroat can grow up to 24 inches (60 centimeters) long. The adult sea-run cutthroat usually weigh from 1 to 4 pounds (0.5 to 1.8 kilograms).

Young cutthroat spend from one to four years in freshwater streams. They spend only about one

year in saltwater before they return to spawn. The adults return to their freshwater streams in the fall and spawn between December and May. Like steelhead, some cutthroat survive spawning, return to the ocean, and return to spawn again the next year.

CHAPTER 6
PEOPLE AND THE COLUMBIA RIVER BASIN

American Indians have lived in the Columbia River Basin for at least ten thousand years. A number of different tribes, including the Chinook, Warm Springs, Nez Perce, Umatilla, and Yakama, lived along the Columbia River and its tributaries.

The Indians caught as many as five million salmon out of the ten to sixteen million that returned to the Columbia River Basin every year. Many tribes had large villages at the best fishing spots along the Columbia and its major tributaries. Salmon were an important food and a vital part of the Indian culture.

In 1792 Captain Robert Gray was the first European to discover the mouth of the Columbia River. He and his crew sailed a few miles up the river and named the river after his ship, *Columbia Rediviva.* They carried iron, copper, buttons, beads, and blue cloth, which they traded with the Indians for furs. Other traders also visited the Columbia River, but none stayed for long.

In 1803 President Thomas Jefferson directed Captains Meriwether Lewis and William

NATIVE AMERICANS FISH AT CELILO FALLS ON THE COLUMBIA RIVER, OREGON, IN 1953.

Clark to lead an exploring party overland to the Pacific Ocean. In 1805 Lewis and Clark traveled down the Snake River to the Columbia and then down the Columbia to the Pacific Ocean. They became the first European American explorers to travel across the entire Columbia River Basin.

Other explorers and fur traders soon followed to the Pacific Northwest. Traders built trading posts and began to live there year-round. By the 1830s, people were realizing that the Columbia River Basin was rich in resources—fish, forests, gold, silver, and good soil for farming. The number of settlers grew rapidly, and towns began to develop in the Willamette Valley and along the Columbia.

In the 1850s, steamboats began to travel the Columbia River, carrying passengers and freight between towns. By the 1870s, railroads were built along the Columbia and throughout the basin. Soon they carried most of the basin's people and freight.

But all these people caused damage to the entire Columbia River ecosystem. Farmers began to draw water out of the Columbia and Snake Rivers and their tributaries to use in irrigation systems. In irrigation farming, water is pumped from a river, lake, or well, through a system of ditches or pipes, to the fields. By the late 1800s, farmers were drawing so much water out of some rivers that the rivers were almost dry during the summer, when most watering was done. Without water in the rivers, the adult salmon could not swim upriver to spawn, and the salmon smolts could not travel downriver to the ocean.

People were also logging in many of the Columbia River Basin's forests. Some logging was done on steep mountainsides, which often caused large amounts of sediment to fall into the streams. Logging greatly increased the number of landslides—more than the ecosystem could absorb. Often when an area was logged, the trees in the riparian areas were cut too. Many streams lost the trees that provided shade, structure, and habitats. Driftwood logs were pulled out of the rivers to make the rivers safer and easier for boats to travel, and logjams were cleared.

Miners found gold and silver in some

parts of the Columbia River Basin. They sometimes dug up large areas of the riverbed to remove gold from the gravel, greatly damaging the structure and habitats of the riverbeds.

People didn't want the rivers to flood their towns, which were situated along the banks. So as towns grew, people forced rivers into one or two main channels, often by building concrete walls along the riverbanks. People removed riparian forests and built roads and buildings right down to the riverbanks. As a result, rivers that flowed through cities were completely cut off from their floodplains and lost most of their structure. Rivers no longer had complex habitats.

People also polluted the water. Some pollution, such as sewage, was poured directly into rivers. Other pollution was poured onto the ground. When pollutants soak into the ground, they continue to soak deeper until they reach the groundwater. Once pollution is in the groundwater, it continues to travel and spread. Eventually it can reach rivers, where it can kill fish and poison the aquatic life.

Because rivers are closely connected to their watersheds, rivers are affected by

LOGGED TREES PILED UP IN A STREAMBED, AWAITING SPRING FLOODS TO CARRY THEM TO THE COLUMBIA RIVER

activities on land. Many human activities affect rivers for a long way downstream, not just the area next to the activity. If a poorly built road causes a lot of sediment to pour into a river, the sediment affects the river until it settles out of the water, which may be many miles downstream. When riparian forests are cut, rivers may erode the riverbanks, and the water may become warmer as shade is lost. Without trees, the riparian soil cannot store as much water. It has little or no water to release to the river during late summer, when the river's water levels drop. By the start of the twentieth century, the Columbia River watershed had been transformed, with enormous effects on the river ecosystem.

Human activities were beginning to impact salmon. The number of salmon returning to the Columbia and its tributaries each year began to drop.

BECAUSE RIVERS ARE CLOSELY CONNECTED TO THEIR WATERSHEDS, RIVERS ARE AFFECTED BY ACTIVITIES ON LAND. MANY HUMAN ACTIVITIES AFFECT RIVERS FOR A LONG WAY DOWNSTREAM, NOT JUST THE AREA NEXT TO THE ACTIVITY.

Farming, logging, and mining were damaging the streams where salmon spawned and salmon fry spent the early part of their lives. People also opened salmon canneries. The fishers began to catch too many of the salmon, not leaving enough fish to spawn and produce the next generation of salmon.

In the 1920s, federal and state governments began planning to build dams across the Columbia River and in other rivers in the Columbia River Basin. People wanted the dams for several reasons: to produce electricity, to control floods, to provide water for irrigation, and to make it easier for large ships to travel on the river.

Dams have been built on the Columbia, the Snake, and other rivers. The first dam built across the Columbia was Rock Island Dam in Washington,

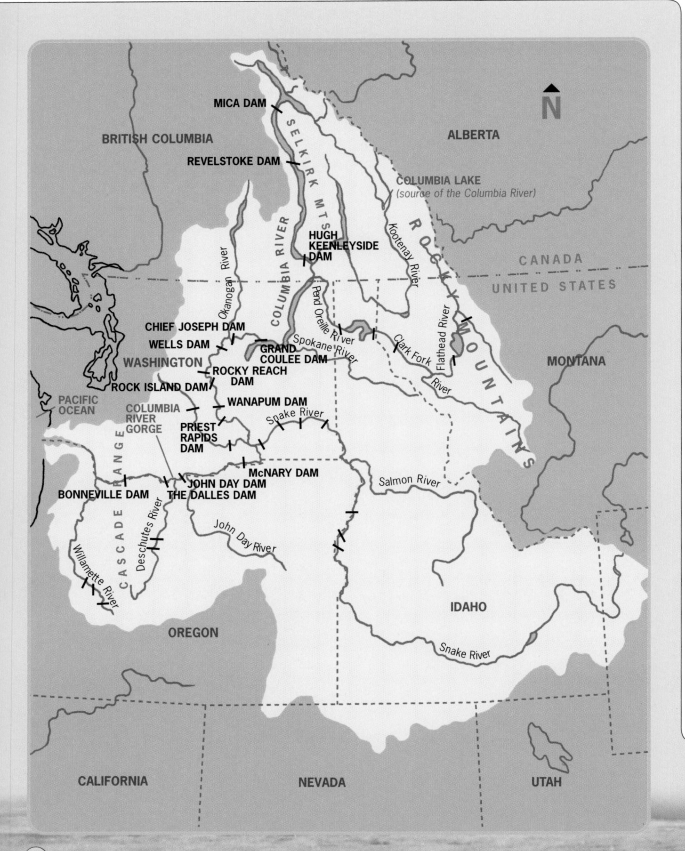

which was completed in 1933. The largest dam, the Grand Coulee in northeastern Washington, was completed in 1941. In all, there are nineteen major dams in the United States portion of the Columbia River Basin, as well as hundreds of other smaller dams throughout the watershed. Almost every tributary river has at least one dam, and many have several dams.

The dams and reservoirs have done a lot of damage to the Columbia River ecosystem. The dams block the ecosystem's normal upstream and downstream movements and processes. The dams prevent fish and other aquatic life from moving freely upstream and downstream. While the water still goes through at a controlled rate, the dams stop driftwood logs from floating downstream. The reservoirs turn parts of the rivers into lakes and replace the complex habitats of rivers with simple habitats that have much less biodiversity. Rivers in the Columbia River Basin no longer run high in the winter and spring. Floods do not occur, so the surrounding land cannot renew itself as well as it once could.

The dams have greatly damaged the salmon runs. Dams have blocked the

GRAND COULEE DAM, WASHINGTON

salmon's access to more than one-third of their habitat in the Columbia River Basin. Grand Coulee Dam alone cut off access to more than 1,000 miles (1,600 kilometers) of salmon habitat. The "June hog" run of chinook salmon, fish that weighed more than 100 pounds (50 kilograms), used to migrate to the upper Columbia River. This salmon stock is now extinct—it has died out—because Grand Coulee Dam blocked its return to its spawning grounds.

At some dams, fish ladders, series of pools built along the side of a dam that look like giant stair steps, allow adult salmon to return upriver. Water flows down through the pools, allowing the adult fish to swim upstream past a dam.

But when salmon smolts migrate downstream, they are unable to reach the fish ladders at the side of the dams. Along with most of the water in the reservoirs, the smolts pass directly through the electric turbines under the dams. The young fish are injured or stunned by the powerful force of the water or they are chopped up by the turbine blades. Ten to thirty percent of the salmon smolts are killed at each dam—and most smolts have to get past several dams.

Dams cause other problems for smolts. The dams' reservoirs slow down the current and hold back the spring runoff, making the smolts' journey to the ocean very difficult. Unlike adult salmon, smolts are too small to swim hundreds of miles. They depend on the river current, especially the spring runoff, to carry them

FISH LADDER AT BONNEVILLE DAM, OREGON

downstream. Snake River salmon runs, for example, have to get past eight dams and their reservoirs, which greatly delay their trip. Most of these smolts are killed before they can reach the ocean.

People have established fish hatcheries as an attempt to help the salmon runs. A fish hatchery is a place where fish biologists hatch fertilized salmon eggs and raise the young fish until they can be released into a river. There are more than eighty fish hatcheries in the Columbia River Basin. While hatcheries succeed in producing salmon, they have problems too. Diseases spread easily in the crowded pens at hatcheries, killing many fish. The fish that survive sometimes spread diseases to wild salmon. Salmon living in a hatchery do not have to find their own food or learn how to escape from predators, so the hatchery fish are less able to survive in natural rivers than the wild salmon.

As a result of human activities, the salmon runs of the Columbia River Basin are a fraction of what they used to be. The annual salmon runs were originally ten to sixteen million fish. They have been reduced to less than two million fish, and most are hatchery bred.

Some salmon stocks are extinct. Many Columbia River Basin salmon runs have been listed as endangered (in danger of going extinct) or threatened (likely to become endangered in the future). The federal government decides which salmon runs to list. Federal scientists classify the many individual salmon runs together into a few bigger groups called units. For example, the "Snake River spring/summer chinook unit" includes chinook runs in the Clearwater, Lochsa, Salmon, and Grande Ronde Rivers, which all flow into the Snake River.

Humans' actions also affected other wildlife of the Columbia River Basin. The peregrine falcon is listed as threatened and the Columbian white-tailed deer is listed as endangered. The Columbian white-tailed deer is a subspecies of the white-tailed deer. These deer were once found throughout the river valleys of the Pacific Northwest. When people settled in the river valleys and cut the riparian forests, the deer lost most of their habitat. They are found only along the lower Columbia River and on one other river in southern Oregon.

THREATENED AND ENDANGERED SALMON AND STEELHEAD IN THE COLUMBIA RIVER BASIN

Year	Salmon or Steelhead Unit	Listing Status
1991	Snake River sockeye	*Endangered*
1992	Snake River spring/summer chinook	*Threatened*
1992	Snake River fall chinook	*Threatened*
1999	Lower Columbia chum	*Threatened*
1999	Lower Columbia spring chinook	*Threatened*
1999	Lower Columbia steelhead	*Threatened*
1999	Upper Willamette steelhead	*Threatened*
1999	Upper Willamette spring chinook	*Threatened*
1999	Middle Columbia steelhead	*Threatened*
1999	Upper Columbia spring chinook	*Endangered*
1999	Upper Columbia steelhead	*Endangered*
1999	Snake River steelhead	*Threatened*

Geographic Area

Salmon River in Idaho, a tributary of the Snake River

Snake River and main tributaries, including Clearwater, Lochsa, Salmon, and Grande Ronde Rivers

Snake River

Lower Columbia River tributaries, up to Columbia Gorge, including Cowlitz River

Lower Columbia River tributaries, up to Columbia Gorge, not including the Willamette watershed

Lower Columbia River tributaries, up to Columbia Gorge, not including the Willamette watershed

Willamette River and tributaries

Willamette watershed, especially McKenzie River

Columbia River tributaries east of Columbia Gorge, especially John Day River

Columbia River tributaries in Northern Washington, especially Okanogan, Methow, and Wenatchee Rivers

Columbia River tributaries in Northern Washington, especially Okanogan, Methow, and Wenatchee Rivers

Snake River and main tributaries

Many other species, like the Columbia pebblesnail, are becoming rare, although the pebblesnail is not yet officially listed as threatened. This snail was once found in the lower and middle Columbia River, and major tributary rivers such as the Snake River. It lives only in a couple of places in the Columbia and Snake Rivers and in some large rivers in Washington, such as the Okanogan River. This snail needs clean, swift-flowing water with a lot of dissolved oxygen and a river bottom of boulders and gravel. But the current can no longer wash sediment downriver, and the rocky river bottoms have become covered with sediment.

Most species of mollusks that live in the Columbia River Basin need cold, clean, fast-flowing water that holds lots of oxygen. This type of habitat is less common, so some species of mollusks have become very rare.

Some species have actually benefited from the changes. Many species of ducks have increased in numbers. The reservoirs provide good habitat for duck, and the edges of the reservoirs provide new wetlands.

COLUMBIAN WHITE-TAILED DEER (*ODOCOILEUS VIRGINIANUS LEUCURUS*)

HELPING THE WILD SALMON AND OTHER COLUMBIA RIVER SPECIES RETURN

People have been working for many years to help the salmon, but many of their projects have failed. The salmon runs continue to decline. Many scientists believe we must follow these basic principles to save the wild salmon.

- Protect the remaining healthy areas in the Columbia River ecosystem first, then work on restoring other areas in the ecosystem.
- Return the rivers to being natural ecosystems, as much as possible. Let riparian areas grow into forests again, let rivers reconnect to parts of their floodplains, and let rivers flow according to their natural patterns.
- Remember that the entire river ecosystem is connected, from headwater streams to large rivers. It is important to think in terms of whole ecosystems and watersheds when trying to solve problems.
- Because each salmon stock is unique, work to keep all of the individual stocks that spawn throughout the Columbia River Basin.

Government agencies, Indian tribes, fishers, businesspeople, and other interested people are looking at ways to help wild salmon by restoring the Columbia River ecosystem. The following are some actions that are being taken in the Columbia River Basin or that will be taken.

- Protecting and restoring habitat in streams. Rules are already in place that require loggers to leave trees in riparian areas. Planned projects will rebuild stream structure, improve water quality, and allow streams to function normally as ecosystems again.
- Releasing water from dams in a way that resembles natural river flows. Before the dams were built, rivers ran high in late spring as the snow melted. The high flows carried salmon smolts to the ocean quickly. If dam operators release more water when salmon need it, more young salmon will survive their journey to the ocean.
- Finding a method for smolts to survive going through dams. Several methods are being tried: screening electric turbines so that smolts don't go through them; spilling more water, and smolts with it, directly

over dams; and carrying smolts around the dams in barges or special trucks.

• Reducing fishing.

• Improving hatchery practices so that hatchery fish do not spread disease to wild fish.

• Protecting good habitat where it already exists.

Many fish biologists recommend breaching, or dismantling, dams, which would allow rivers to run wild again. The idea of breaching four federal dams on the lower Snake River is being discussed. This would help the Snake River salmon runs, but it would mean losing the electric power generated by those dams. Also, without the reservoirs, barges could no longer travel up and down the Snake River. Wheat and other goods would have to be moved by trains or trucks instead. People need to decide how much they are willing to give up in order to save the salmon.

While work to help the wild salmon has not been successful so far, efforts to protect some other threatened or endangered species of wildlife have been successful. National wildlife refuges throughout the Columbia River Basin provide safe areas for many species, including bald eagles, deer, ospreys, great blue herons, ducks, geese, and seabirds. The bald eagle was listed as a threatened species for many years, but the number of bald eagles has grown so much that the species was removed from the threatened list in 1999. Along the lower Columbia River, the Columbian white-tailed deer is protected in a refuge, and its numbers are slowly growing.

WILLAMETTE NATIONAL FOREST, OREGON

WHAT YOU CAN DO

PROTECTING RIVER ECOSYSTEMS

We are all involved with the fate of the wild salmon and other aquatic species. We all live in watersheds, and many things that we do every day affect river ecosystems. You can help to restore the health of the Columbia River (if you live in the Pacific Northwest) or the health of the river that flows through your watershed. Here are some things you can do to protect river ecosystems:

• Never pour motor oil, gasoline, paint, household cleaners, or other chemicals down the sink, into a toilet, onto the ground, into a storm drain, or into a river. These chemicals can kill fish directly by poisoning them. They can also kill fish indirectly by polluting the water, killing the small plants and animals that fish eat, or creating a film on the water that prevents oxygen from getting into the water. Just 1 quart (0.9 liter) of oil can contaminate 250,000 gallons (950,000 liters) of water.

If oil, gas, or chemicals are poured down a sink or flushed down a toilet, they go into either a septic system or a city sewer system. These systems are not designed to clean chemicals out of the water, so the chemicals end up in a river somewhere. If chemicals are poured onto the ground, they soak down into the ground. Eventually, these chemicals can reach the groundwater and travel underground into the river. Storm drains are the drains along city streets that rainwater runs into. These drains go directly to a river without going through a water treatment plant, so any chemicals poured into these drains go directly into the river.

• Some gas stations accept used motor oil. In some cities and towns, there are special collection sites for chemicals. And some cities have one or two days each year when garbage collectors accept hazardous waste such as these chemicals.

• Keep trash and litter out of rivers. Some communities have an annual river clean-up day or beach clean-up day, when people volunteer to help local agencies pick up all trash along a stretch of river or beach. Volunteers working together have picked up tons of trash in one day.

- Leave trees, bushes, and other vegetation that are growing along riverbanks. The roots of trees and bushes help to hold the riverbank in place when the river runs high. Trees and bushes also help to shade the river, keeping the water cool. Plants along the water's edge provide shelter for small fish. On land, trees and bushes provide habitat for animals that live in riparian zones.

- Help plant trees and bushes along riverbanks. In some towns, groups have formed to take care of their local rivers. Many groups have a tree planting day in the spring. The group provides the trees and shovels.

- Conserve electricity. Turn lights off when you don't need them, use a little less heat in the winter, and use less air conditioning in the summer. If we conserve electricity, government agencies can spill more water over dams and let more spring runoff out of the reservoirs. These actions help salmon smolts get downriver more quickly and safely.

- It's OK to eat salmon. All commercial fishing for salmon is carefully regulated by federal and state fishing agencies, in order to prevent overfishing on salmon stocks that need protection. Some salmon stocks in Canada and Alaska are still very healthy, and fishers are allowed to catch some of those fish. Much of the salmon in stores and restaurants comes from salmon "ranches," where salmon are raised in net pens in saltwater.

WHAT HAPPENS IN THE FUTURE? YOU CAN BE INVOLVED

Many people are involved in making the decisions about what should be done to help wild salmon and to restore the Columbia River ecosystem. Most of these people work in the federal and state governments or with the Indian tribes. Congress and the president make decisions about laws affecting the Columbia River Basin. Government agencies such as Bonneville Power Administration and the Army Corps of Engineers make decisions about how the dams are operated. The National Marine Fisheries Service decides whether a salmon run is threatened or endangered. Other agencies decide how hatcheries are operated and how much fishing is allowed. All of these people consider the views of the public when they make their decisions.

If you live in the Pacific Northwest, you'll see news about the Columbia River salmon runs and dams and about decisions being made about how to manage them. Find out all you can about proposed laws and plans for the rivers in the Columbia River Basin. Read newspapers and magazines to learn more. Once you have decided what you think about the plans that are being made, write a letter to your state senator or representative. Tell them your views on the best ways to manage the Columbia River for people and for salmon. Here are some addresses you can use.

To write to the president:
The President
The White House
Washington, D.C. 20500

To write to the senators from your state:
The Honorable (name of your senator)
United States Senate
Washington, D.C. 20510

To write to your representative in Congress:
The Honorable (name of your representative)
U.S. House of Representatives
Washington, D.C. 20515

WEBSITES TO VISIT FOR MORE INFORMATION

Many government agencies and nonprofit groups have websites with more information about the Columbia River Basin and the wild salmon. Just a few of these websites are listed below.

American Rivers

<http://www.amrivers.org>

American Rivers is a nonprofit group that works to protect and restore rivers all over the country. Their website has information about their campaigns to restore the Columbia River Basin, the rivers Lewis and Clark traveled, and other rivers.

Bonneville Power Administration

<http://www.bpa.gov>

The Bonneville Power Administration is the federal agency that sells the electricity generated by the federal dams in the Columbia River Basin. Their website has information on the environment, fish and other wildlife of the basin, and government programs to restore the environment in the basin.

The Columbia River Inter-Tribal Fisheries Commission

<http://www.critfc.org>

The Columbia River Inter-Tribal Fisheries Commission represents four Columbia River tribes. Their website has information on Columbia River Basin salmon, the tribal vision for the future of the basin, and tribal projects to restore salmon.

For the Sake of the Salmon

<http://www.4sos.org>

For the Sake of the Salmon is a nonprofit group working to restore salmon. Their website has information on salmon biology and restoring and protecting salmon habitat.

Inforain

<http://www.inforain.org/interactivemapping/salmonstock.htm>

Inforain is a project of the nonprofit organization Ecotrust. Their website has maps of Columbia River Basin salmon stocks.

Pacific Rivers Council

<http://www.pacrivers.org>

The Pacific Rivers Council is a nonprofit

group that works to conserve and restore all rivers along the Pacific Coast and in the Columbia River Basin. Their website explains their conservation programs, including "Salmon-Safe," and projects for the Columbia River Basin.

FOR FURTHER READING

Bramwell, Martyn. *Rivers and Lakes*. New York: Franklin Watts, 1994.

Duden, Jane. *Floods! Rising, Raging Waters*. Logan, Iowa: Perfection Learning Corporation, 1999.

Hirschi, Ron. *Salmon*. Minneapolis: Carolrhoda Books, 2001.

Hoff, Mary, and Mary M. Rodgers. *Our Endangered Planet: Rivers and Lakes*. Minneapolis: Lerner Publications Company, 1991.

Martin, Patricia A. Fink. *Rivers and Streams*. New York: Franklin Watts, Inc., 1999.

McClung, Robert M. *Lost Wild America: The Story of Our Extinct and Vanishing Wildlife*. Hamden, Connecticut: Linnet Books, 1993.

Mudd-Ruth, Maria. *The Mississippi River*. New York: Benchmark Books, 2001.

Patent, Dorothy Hinshaw. *Biodiversity*. New York: Clarion Books, 1996.

Sauvain, Philip. *Rivers and Valleys*. Minneapolis: Carolrhoda Books, 1996.

Sayre, April Pulley. *River and Stream*. New York: Twenty-First Century Books, 1996.

Scott, Michael. *Ecology*. New York: Oxford University Press, 1995.

VanCleave, Janice. *Ecology for Every Kid: Easy Activities That Make Learning About Science Fun*. New York: John Wiley & Sons, 1996.

Walker, Sally M. *Water Up, Water Down: The Hydrologic Cycle*. Minneapolis: Carolrhoda Books, 1992.

Waters, Thomas F. *Wildstream: A Natural History of the Free Flowing River*. Saint Paul, Minnesota: Riparian Press, 2000.

Whitman, Sylvia. *This Land Is Your Land: The American Conservation Movement*. Minneapolis: Lerner Publications Company, 1994.

GLOSSARY

alevin: a newly hatched salmon still wearing a yolk sac

algae: simple plants or plantlike organisms that grow in water or on damp surfaces

anadromous fish: a fish that hatches in freshwater, grows to adulthood in the ocean, and returns to streams and rivers to lay eggs

aquatic: having to do with water; living in or on water

biodiversity: the number of different species of plants and animals living in an area

composition: the different species of plants, animals, fungi, and bacteria that live in an ecosystem

decay: to break down

decomposers: organisms that break down plant and animal matter into simple nutrients that can be used again by plants

endangered: in danger of becoming extinct

erosion: the process in which flowing water wears away soil and rock

estuary: the wide part of a river where freshwater meets and mixes with saltwater

floodplains: flat areas covered with sediment left behind by receding floodwaters

fry: young salmon that have absorbed their yolk sac and must hunt for food

functions: activities and processes that go on in an ecosystem. Functions include birth, growth, reproduction, death, and decay.

groundwater: water that is under the ground

habitat: the kind of environment in which a species normally lives

headwaters: the source of a river or stream

irrigation: moving water from a river or lake to farm fields

larvae: insects in an early stage of their development

logjams: jumbles of logs piled up together in streams or rivers

meander: to wander back and forth

milt: the sperm-containing fluid of a male fish

photosynthesis: the process by which green plants use sunlight, carbon dioxide, and water to make their own food

primary consumers: plant-eating animals

primary producers: green plants that make the foods that they need to grow

redd: a salmon's nest in the gravel of a stream

reservoirs: artificial lakes that form behind dams

riparian area: the land close to a river

runoff: the part of a heavy rain that runs into rivers or streams, often carrying soil, leaves, or other material with it

secondary consumers: animals that eat plant-eating animals. Secondary consumers are also called predators.

sediment: soil, leaves, and other materials carried into streams by rain, floods, or landslides

smolt: young salmon just going to sea, usually recognized by their bright silver color

spawn: to lay eggs

stock: a local population of a salmon species that migrates to a particular river or lake at a specific season in order to spawn. Willamette River spring chinook and Snake River fall chinook are two examples of salmon stocks.

structures: the physical parts of an ecosystem, such as rocks and logs

terraces: raised areas of land alongside rivers

terrestrial: having to do with the land

threatened: likely to become endangered in the future

tributaries: streams or rivers that flow into a larger river

water table: the top of the part of the ground that is soaked with water. The water table may be deep underground or right at the surface.

watershed: an area of land from which water drains into a particular river or stream

INDEX

ABOUT THE AUTHOR

Valerie Rapp is a science writer. She is the winner of a 1996 fellowship in nonfiction from Literary Arts, Inc., in Oregon. Valerie has worked in natural resource management since 1978. In addition to writing scientific and technical publications about forests, rivers, and watersheds, she has had jobs in wildland firefighting, trail work, timber sale planning, and wild and scenic river planning.

She has a B.A. in English literature from the University of Buffalo, New York. She lives with her husband, Gene Skrine, in Portland, Oregon. Three stepchildren are also an important part of her family.

Her book *What the River Reveals: Understanding and Restoring Healthy Watersheds* explains how we've changed our rivers in the Pacific Northwest and what we can do to restore our rivers and watersheds. In all her writing, she focuses on the complex relationships between people and nature.

PHOTO ACKNOWLEDGEMENTS

The photographs in this book are reproduced with the permission of: © Gary Schultz, pp. 2–3, p. 36, 40 (left), 43, 47 (bottom); © Maxine Cass, p. 9; © Gary Braasch, pp. 11, 16, 18, 20, 21, 32 (top), 34, 46 (bottom); © Linda J. Moore, pp. 14, 15 (left), 25, 44, 48, 60; © Fred Gebhart, p. 15 (right); © Michael P. Gadomski/Photo Researchers, Inc., p. 22; © William Grenfall/Visuals Unlimited, p. 23; © Daniel D. Lamoreaux/Visuals Unlimited, p. 29; © Jack Ballard/Visuals Unlimited, p. 32 (bottom); © Art Wolf/Photo Researchers, Inc., p. 33; © Roger Klocek/Visuals Unlimited, p. 38 (left); © Charlie Heidecker/Visuals Unlimited, p. 38 (right); © Glen Oliver/Visuals Unlimited, pp. 40 (right), 41 (left); © Patrice/Visuals Unlimited, p. 41 (right); © Tom & Pat Leeson/Photo Researchers, Inc., pp. 46 (top), 47 (top), 49 (top); Pt. Defiance Aquarium, Tacoma, © Tom McHugh/Photo Researchers, Inc., p. 49 (bottom); Oregon Historical Society, p. 50 (OrHi 93717), 52 (ORH.4698); © Ted Clutter/Photo Researchers, Inc., p. 55; © Rita Nannini/Photo Researchers, Inc., p. 56; USDA Forest Service, p. 63. Maps and illustrations on pp. 8, 13, 17, and 54 by Tim Seeley. Bottom border by Adam Lerner/IPS. Cover photograph © Gary Schultz.